Peepa's Purple Soup

Written By

Bill Medeiros

Illustrated by

Sarah Medeiros

2023

Dedication

This book is dedicated to my Uncle (Tio) Jose de Medeiros for bringing the fruit of the vine from the Azores to the backyards of Somerville, Massachusetts and the skills he handed down to my family which produced decades of bounty for the enjoyment of many. To my parents and in-laws for keeping the tradition long enough for a son to keep it alive in his hometown.

Acknowledgments

I want to give thanks to the special people behind this project. My good friend Steven H. Manchester for his gracious time, incredible talent and dedicated effort in assisting me through my first literary endeavor. His commitment to my success in completing this book is priceless. To my neighbor, Linda Cornell, who gave of her time and editorial talent in combing through many drafts and helped me craft my words with brevity and clarity. My daughter, Sarah, who through her artistic ability captured the characters' personalities. My wife, Maria, who drew from her career as an elementary school teacher, guided my storytelling with the reader in mind. Above all, I give glory and thanks to my God and Savior who blessed me with children and grandchildren.

Going to Mimi's

It was a crisp autumn Saturday morning in New England. Olivia found herself staying in bed an extra-long time. Looking out the window, she saw big maple trees full of bright yellow, orange, and crimson red leaves.

"Olivia, are you going to get up, or should we leave without you on our surprise trip?" Her mother asked as she entered Olivia's room.

Still sleepy, Olivia sat up and snuggled next to her mom, sitting on the edge of the bed.

Olivia asked, "What special trip?"

"Well, Dad and I were thinking about spending the day at Mimi and Peepa's house. But since you're not ready, maybe, just maybe, we won't go."

"What!" Olivia cried out. "Who said I wasn't ready!" She leaped out of bed, flying down the hallway like a rocket. Minutes later, Olivia dressed and directed the whole family into the van. They were off to the city to visit Olivia's grandparents.

Olivia was becoming lost in thought while staring out the van's window.

Her mom looked over her shoulder and noticed her daughter's expression. "Olivia, is there something wrong, honey?"

Olivia responded, "Well, I was just wondering what goodies Mimi might have for me."

"What do you mean for you?" her older brother Cameron asked. "I bet she has a nice plate of rice pudding waiting for her favorite grandson. Yum."

Olivia looked at her brother, "I don't think so, Cam. It's not Thanksgiving, so it's way too early for that. I bet its cookies!"

Elena woke up at the word "cookies," her eyes twinkling.

"Maybe your grandmother has some nice soup warming up on the stove," Dad said from behind the steering wheel.

"Stoup," Elena cried out from her car seat. "Yucko!"

Everyone in the car laughed at Elena's reaction.

The debate on what Mimi might have waiting for them continued all the way to Mimi and Peepa's driveway. Once the van engine turned off, Olivia wasted no time getting the upper hand on her brother. Unbuckling her seatbelt and jumping out of the van, she cried, "Ha, whatever Mimi has, I'm having it first!"

"Hey! No fair!" complained Cameron. "Who said she gets firsties?"

Cameron could hear Olivia gleefully exclaiming, "It's all for me!" as she ran up the front walkway to the porch.

"Mimi! Cookies!" Cried Elena. While helping Elena out of her car seat, Cam could only think, "How does that girl get her way all the time? She better not be sticking her fingers in Mimi's rice pudding."

Vovó,[1] Olivia's great-grandmother and Mimi's mother, who lived on the first floor, opened the front door just as Olivia came bursting through it, making a beeline up the stairs to see Mimi. Her great-grandmother cried out, "What is this? No kisses for Vovó."

Olivia called back as she scampered up the stairs, "Vovó! I'll be down soon!"

Standing in the middle of her kitchen, hearing all the commotion, Mimi called out into the hallway, "What is going on out there?" Knowing all the time the source of the clamor coming up the stairs.

_____
[1] An informal Portuguese term for grandmother pronounced as "vuhvaw."

Where's Peepa?

"Mimi!" Olivia exclaimed as she ran into her grandmother's arms. But Mimi refused to let her go. Peeking through her grandmother's hug, Olivia started searching the counter for goodies. She spotted a plate of Mimi's rice pudding, which was Cam's favorite. But she smelled something else, and her mouth started watering.

"Hey, Mimi, I smell something I like," she said, looking toward the oven.

"Well, little girl," said Mimi, "you're going to have to wait because I just put them in the oven."

With a smirk on her face and a twinkle in her eye, Olivia sighed, "Well, okay, if you say so." Olivia knew they were chocolate chip cookies.

Where is Peepa?" Olivia asked.

Her grandmother replied, "I think he's outside. Go look out the window." Mimi pointed toward the family room.

Olivia skipped into the family room to see Auntie Sarah sitting on the sofa with her sketch pad. Olivia hopped onto the sofa beside her aunt and asked, "Auntie Sarah, have you seen Peepa?"

"Keep looking. You'll see him," her aunt pointed out the window above the sofa.

Olivia looked out the window, wondering, "Where is Peepa." She then spotted him busy under the grapevines. "Hey Peepa," she hollered out the open window, "what are you doing?"

Hearing the familiar voice, her grandfather looked around. Olivia was nowhere to be found. He stepped out from under the vines and looked at the second-floor window. "There you are, Livey. What a nice surprise," he said. "What am I doing? I'm pruning the grapevines."

To Olivia's surprise, her grandfather was cutting branches off the vines. Some cuttings were very long, leaving only short branches on the vines. "Oh no!" she thought. "He needs to stop cutting them."

He's Destroying Them!

Olivia leaped off the couch and flew out of the family room. She grabbed the kitchen door to the back stairs and cried, "He's going to destroy them!"

As she stormed down the back stairs, Mimi called out, "Who is going to destroy what?"

Olivia responded, "It's Peepa! He's going to destroy the grapevines! Mimi, he needs to stop!"

Mimi stood at the top of the stairs and asked, "Livey, what about the cookies?"

Olivia waved her hands as if stopping traffic. "Don't let Cam or Elena have any of my cookies before I come back!" She instructed her grandmother. With that, she spun around, opened the porch door, and headed down the stairs to the backyard.

"Peepa, what are you doing?" Olivia asked, with a look of horror on her face. She grabbed her grandfather's hand and yanked on it like a tugboat pulling on a ship.

"Livey, Livey, what's wrong?" Asked Peepa.

"Look at what you're doing, Peepa. You're going to destroy the grapevines!" Olivia said, pointing to the grapevines on the trellis overhead.

Peepa held back his laughter. He knelt, holding her hands, trying to calm her. "Olivia, why would I destroy the grapevines when I work so hard to keep going what Vovó and Vovô[2] have been caring for many years? Not just them, but my uncle brought some over from Portugal a long time ago." Olivia listened as Peepa explained that grapevines, whether small or great, need

_____
[2] Informal Portuguese terms for grandmother and grandfather are pronounced as "vohvaw" and "vohvoo."

to be trimmed back to get bigger and stronger. "Livey, I can't make my purple soup if I don't trim the grapevines," Peepa explained as he returned to his pruning.

Olivia turned around and walked up the stairs into the house, making her way back to the kitchen. Looking confused, she shook her head. With her hands on her cheeks, Olivia asked her grandmother, "Mimi, I thought you were the soup maker in this house?"

"I am Sweety, with some help from Vovó. Why do you ask?"

"Peepa said he needed to cut the branches off the grapevine to make his purple soup," Olivia said sadly. "All he has down there is a pile of sticks."

"Oh, Livey, I am sure your Peepa isn't making any soup with a pile of dead grapevine branches. Now, what about those cookies?"

No Purple Soup for Peepa

Weeks later, Olivia slowly got out of bed and looked out the window to see the first snowfall. Her mom called down the hallway. "Hey Olivia, Mimi called and invited us for the afternoon. Are you up for some Thanksgiving Day leftovers?"

"I am. Let's go!" shouted Cam from his bedroom.

Olivia thought, "I wonder if Auntie Sarah, Auntie Jessica, and Peepa ate all those pies from the other day? Hmmm, maybe I can get Mimi to make some chocolate pudding?"

The family got ready, piled into the van, and went off to Somerville.

Later, they all sat in the family room, sharing stories and playing games. Mimi snuck out to the kitchen to prepare another delicious meal.

"Come and get it!" Mimi called from the dining room. Everybody started making their way out of the family room through the kitchen and into the dining room – everyone except Olivia.

Peepa turned around and noticed Olivia looking out the window, deep in thought.

"Livey, aren't you hungry? Is there something wrong, Sweety?" Asked Peepa.

Olivia didn't even turn around when she responded, keeping her gaze out the window. "Peepa, it sure doesn't look like you're going to be making any purple soup. Your sticks and branches are gone, and the grapevines are covered in snow. What are you going to do?"

He walked back into the family room and sat down next to Olivia, "Sweety, I'm just going to have to wait on God's timing."

"What does God have to do with your purple soup?" she quizzed him.

"I have no control over the weather or the grapevines coming back to life. And by the way, the sticks have nothing to do with the soup," he said, chuckling. "But since we have to wait, let's fill our bellies with the scrumptious food Mimi has prepared for us. The last one to the table gets no pie for dessert!"

Olivia shot out of the family room, making her way to the table with the rest of the family.

Spring, Soccer, and Baby Grapes

Christmas, New Year's Day, and winter break, as did the winter snows, came and went.

At last, spring arrived. Olivia was back on the soccer practice field wearing her uniform. She was tired at the end of her first game but not too tired to brag about the goals she scored. "Hey, Mom," Olivia called out, "do you have your tablet?"

"Why would I bring that to your soccer game? You must have a special reason for me to have it," Mom said, raising an eyebrow.

"Well, I think Mimi is waiting for an update on my soccer game. And I have a question I've been waiting to ask Peepa for a long time," Olivia replied.

"You do, huh?" Mom responded. "Well, since you put it that way, let me check." As they sat on the grass, Mom reached into her carry bag and pulled out her laptop. Olivia watched her mother make a video call to Mimi.

"Hello, who is calling, please?" Olivia heard Mimi's voice as she saw Mimi's face appear on Mom's laptop.

"Mimi, can't you see it's me? You're not going to believe what happened today!" Olivia could hardly contain her excitement. "I scored not just one but two goals!"

"Wow!" shouted Peepa, as his face shifted into view on Mimi's cell phone. "It sounds like I need to call the U.S. Olympic Team officials and tell them about my superstar granddaughter."

Olivia's mother reminded her she had something important to ask her granddad.

"Peepa, Peepa, I have a question for you," she said, catching her grandfather by surprise.

"Oh, you do," he said. "What is it?"

"Are you still waiting on God's timing?" Olivia asked, thinking Peepa had forgotten what he'd told her the day snow was covering his backyard.

"Ah, very good. You remembered. I sure am, and I have a surprise for you." Peepa took Mimi's cell phone, went down the back stairs, and walked out under the grapevines. "Look at this, Livey." He reached out and held a cluster of baby grapes in his hand.

"Peepa, will those grow to be big grapes?" Olivia asked.

"They sure will and so will all the others." Peepa stepped back, showing all the other clusters popping out through the vines.

Amazed, Olivia whispered softly, "wwwoooowwww!"

Summer, Cousins, Cookouts, and Backyard Invaders

Olivia and Cam were out of school for summer vacation. Olivia couldn't wait to see her cousins from North Carolina, who visited every summer. One morning Olivia walked into the kitchen, looked up at her father, and asked, "Daddy, when are we finally going to see Safiyya, Leena, and Ibrahim?"

"You will see them today!" Dad answered. "We're going to Mimi and Peepa's for a nice cookout with your cousins."

"Whoopee!! Let's go!" shouted Olivia.

That afternoon, everyone was sitting at the picnic table under cover of the grapevines. Olivia was enjoying a hamburger.

Looking up, she was surprised to see a squirrel on the back fence stretching over to grab some grapes. "Peepa!" she shouted. "A squirrel is stealing your grapes! Get him."

"Livey, relax, girl," chuckled her grandpa. "Trust me; he won't be taking too many because the grapes are still too green. Also, they're not my grapes. I'm only the caretaker." He winked at his grandchildren, leaving them puzzled about what he really meant.

Leena then looked up and saw birds in the grapevines. "Look, the birds are robbing the grapes, along with the squirrels."

Their grandfather looked over his glasses at Leena and Olivia. "Really, girls? You know we always have birds nesting in the backyard. The robins nest up under the roof of the back porch. Mockingbirds are nesting in the grapevines."

Olivia's cousin Ibrahim asked his father, Baba, "Can you hold me up so I can see it," pointing to the nest above. Baba slowly lifted him, and Ibrahim peeked into the grapevine. He saw the bird's nest with eggs in it.

"Would you like your neighbors to ask you to leave your homes because you were living in their neighborhood?" asked Peepa, looking at his grandchildren.

"No way," said some of the grandchildren.

"Well, what right do Mimi and I have to get rid of the birds' nests? Who should be protecting the little birds?" asked Peepa.

"Isn't that really God's job?" asked Leena's sister, Safiyya.

"And who blessed your grandfather so I could take care of this house along with the backyard and everything that's in the backyard?" he asked.

"Hmmm, I see what you mean, Peepa," Safiyya responded. "I suppose God has put you in charge of that."

Summer Ends, School Starts, and No Purple Soup

Olivia's cousins returned home to North Carolina, and the weeks sped by. Summer break was coming to an end, and the new school year was just around the corner. There would be new teachers, new classmates, and friends and teachers she'd met from the previous school year.

Olivia was in her bedroom looking at her school supplies, thinking how exciting second grade might be. Suddenly, she heard voices down the hallway. She walked into the dining room and saw Mom talking with Mimi and Peepa on the tablet.

She crawled between her mom and the table to get front and center on the video call with her grandparents. "Mimi, Peepa!" exclaimed Olivia. "What are you doing?"

"Hi, Livey," both grandparents responded. "We're just checking in to see how you and Cam are getting ready for a new school year," said Mimi.

"Oh, boy!" piped up Olivia excitedly. "Mom and I went to the store the other day, and it was soooo crazy. I couldn't believe it. It was like a zoo!" Olivia was so excited she was waving her arms and bouncing around like popcorn in a microwave oven.

Her grandfather brought his face right up to the phone's camera and raised his eyebrow like a news reporter. "Are you telling me, Miss Olivia, there were wild animals in the store with all those people shopping?" asked Peepa, pretending to be serious.

"No, Peepa. There you go again, being silly," said Olivia, knowing Peepa sometimes made silly statements. She could hear Mimi telling him not to be such a tease.

"It seemed like a zoo with all the kids, moms, and dads going up and down the aisles grabbing supplies off the shelves," she said, puffing out her chest and tilting her head as if she had won a great prize. "I think Mom and I did an excellent job on our shopping adventure. Wait 'til you see my stuff, Mimi," shouted Olivia. She heard Mimi's response, "I can't wait, Livey."

Suddenly, Mimi's face disappeared, and she saw Peepa's legs and feet walking out of the room, down a set of stairs, and out to the backyard.

Olivia could only hear Peepa saying. "Speaking of seeing stuff, Livey, let me show you my stuff." Next, Olivia saw the grapes on the vines come into view. They were much bigger since the last time she was in his backyard. Some were no longer green.

"Hey Peepa, I thought you said those grapes were God's stuff and not yours?" She said like a schoolteacher correcting a student.

Peepa responded, "Well, I suppose you're right, Livey. I am just the caretaker."

Not letting Peepa off the hook, she continued, "Those grapes are changing, but it looks like you may be "running out of time with God's schedule," reminding her grandfather of the things he told her back in the spring.

"We will have to just wait and see," said Peepa.

After reminding one another how much they loved each other, they ended the video call.

Olivia looked up at her mother with a troubled look in her eyes and said. "How in the world is Peepa going to make purple soup with all those green grapes?"

"As he said, we are going to have to wait and see," her mother responded, smiling at her daughter. Turning around, Olivia walked back to her bedroom shaking her head, thinking her grandfather may be confused about when his grapes would be ready.

They Stole the Grapes!

Olivia was so busy with school, after-school programs, and fall basketball that she forgot Peepa's plans to make his purple soup. One early Sunday afternoon after church service, Olivia's parents decided to swing by Somerville on their way home from Boston. Olivia walked into her grandparent's house and up the stairs while hastily shouting down the staircase to her great-grandmother, "Hi, Vovó."

Nobody was there to greet her. Disappointed, she walked into the family room to find it empty of grandparents and aunties. Walking to the open window, she cried out, "Hey! Where is everybody?"

"I'm right here, Livey," Mimi answered from the kitchen. "Didn't you see me? You walked right by me."

"Really? You must have been hiding in the closet. By the way, where's Peepa?" Olivia asked as she made her way to the window. A warm autumn breeze was blowing through the window, bringing a smile of pleasure to her face. She closed her eyes, wishing the summer would come back just for a few more days. Opening her eyes, she glanced out the window to the neighboring houses.

Olivia looked down at the grapevines and suddenly let a shriek that could be heard from miles away. "Mimi, you've been robbed!" She bolted out of the family room, flung open the kitchen door, and dashed down the stairs shouting over and over, "They robbed you!"

Her grandmother looked down the back stairway, wondering what in the world had gotten into that girl again. "Who is stealing what?" asked Mimi.

"Those squirrels and birds!" cried Olivia as she made her way out to the back porch. Turning back at Mimi, she said, "I told Peepa they have been waiting to make their move since the family cookout!" She spun around and bolted down to the backyard.

Mimi turned around to see her son and daughter-in-law walking into the kitchen. Looking at them, she sighed, "Someday, that girl will give me a heart attack."

Olivia's parents looked at each other – wondering what that girl had done now.

Olivia was running around frantically in the backyard, anticipating the furry and feathered thieves making their last strike. "Peepa, where are you?" She cried out while looking up at the grapevines that were stripped of almost all the grapes. Most of the remaining grapes were partly eaten. "They're coming back to take the last of the grapes." In her mind, she could see an army of squirrels ready to invade the grapevines from the top of the rear fence, calling down a squadron of squawking blue jays. "Peepa, where are you?" She cried.

From the open basement door, Olivia heard, "Olivia Rodgers, why in the world are you carrying on like that?"

"Peepa, don't you see what has happened to the grapevines?" She responded frantically, losing all hope of saving the grapes. Peepa stood looking down over his glasses, shaking his head. "Peepa, didn't you see what the birds and squirrels have done to the grapevines in YOUR backyard?"

Her grandfather took off his glasses, tucked them in his shirt pocket, and stooped over, putting his hands on his granddaughter's shoulders. He looked at Olivia, waiting for her to catch her breath. "Livey," he explained, "of course, I know about the grapevines in MY backyard. And no, it wasn't the birds nor the squirrels."

"It wasn't?" Olivia said, confused. "Then who took them?" she demanded like a crime investigator.

"It was me," replied Peepa. He walked into the basement to the refrigerator and opened the door. "Come and see!"

Olivia walked over and peered into the refrigerator. To her surprise, she saw pots and large pans filled with grapes. "Where did you buy all those grapes?" she asked.

"Buy them? I didn't buy any. Look closely. Don't you see the stems? I was the one who 'ROBBED' the grapevines," chuckled her granddad. "Now, can we go upstairs and see what Mimi has on the dinner table to fill our empty bellies."

"Peepa. I feel much better now." She slapped her grandfather on the arm and ran for the staircase, yelling, "Last one up the stairs is a rotten grape."

Looking for a Helper

Two days later, Olivia's mother received a video call. Mom called out, "Olivia, are you finished with your schoolwork?"

"Yeee-aaa-hhh. You know I did, Mom," came the response from the girl's bedroom.

"Then, you should come out here. I believe someone's looking for you," Mom said.

Olivia left her bedroom and asked, "Who's looking for me?"

Mom directed Olivia's attention to the dining room table, where she saw Mimi on the screen. "Oh, hi, Mimi. Are you looking for me?"

"Not exactly, but if you give me a minute, I can take you to someone who is," she said.

Her grandma's cell phone appeared floating out of the room and down a flight of stairs. "Hey, Mimi, it looks like you're taking me down to the basement," spouted Olivia.

"You're right, Livey. Just give me a minute," replied Mimi.

Mom leaned over her daughter's shoulder and whispered into her ear, "I think it's Peepa who is looking for you."

"Yup, only Peepa likes spending time in the basement," giggled Olivia. "Peepa must be in the basement if he's not upstairs or outside."

There he was, sitting on a stool with a pot filled with clusters of grapes to his left. In front of him was a pot with little green globs and, to his right, a pan with green and purple grape skins. He looked up at Mimi, who was pointing her cell phone toward him so he could see Olivia.

"Hi, Peepa. Are you looking for me?" Olivia asked. "What are you doing?"

"Yes, I am looking for you. I'm separating the grape pulp, the green globs, from their grape skins so I can make my purple soup."

"But all the grape pulp looks green, and not all the skins are purple?" Olivia said, worried.

"Don't worry. I just need a helper in the kitchen this weekend. Do you want to help me?" Asked Peepa.

Olivia looked at her mom and whispered, "Can I help Peepa, Mom? I think he needs me."

"I'm sure he's hoping you will help him," answered Mom.

Olivia swung around and, looking into her mom's tablet, shouted, "You bettcha, Peepa!"

"Alright, my special helper. I'll see you this weekend," he said, ending the call.

Making a Purple Mess!

Olivia's week at school came to an end. She and her family were heading to Mimi and Peepa's on Saturday afternoon. She was going to have a sleepover at her grandparent's house because she had promised to be Peepa's helper. She greeted her great-grandparents at the door and marched upstairs like a soldier of the grapes on a mission. In the kitchen, she saw large plastic bowls filled with grape skins on the counter, and on the stove was a large pan filled with grape pulp. It looked like green jelly eyes since the seeds were still in the little blobs of grape pulp.

Mimi stood next to Olivia. "I'm leaving you two in charge of the kitchen while I go downstairs to help your Vovó and Vovô."

Olivia saluted her grandmother like an obedient soldier, "Yes, General Mimi!" She giggled, trying to keep a serious look on her face.

Mimi leaned over and whispered into her granddaughter's ear. "You make sure Peepa doesn't make a big mess in my kitchen."

Peepa was stirring the pot of grape pulp on the stove and, without looking at either one of them, said, "Don't think I didn't hear that." He chuckled, "Me, make a mess? Impossible!"

Olivia looked at Mimi, whispering with a big smile, "I'll watch him like a hawk."

Nodding, Mimi winked before leaving the kitchen for her parents' apartment downstairs.

"Hey, Peepa!" shouted Olivia. "Let's get busy. What can I do to help?"

"Glad you asked," answered Peepa. "See that bowl of skins on the counter? I need you to put them into the blender on the mixing table I prepared for you. Once you do that, the skins can be pureed. While you're doing that, I'll work on getting the grape pulp ready to be separated from the seeds. Think you can handle that?" he asked.

"That sounds super easy. Of course, I can handle that," said Olivia with great confidence. She stood in front of a small table prepared just for her. She was busy scooping chunks of grape skins into the blender as her grandfather had instructed.

"Now, Livey, don't fill the blender to the top. Remember, Mimi doesn't want any accidents," he warned her.

"Peepa, I'm always a good helper around the kitchen. All you need to do is ask Mom and Dad. "Olivia kept scooping away, adding as many grape skins as possible, squeezing them into the blender. "Okay, which button do I press?" she asked, forgetting to put the lid on tight.

Looking to his left, Peepa immediately knew a catastrophe was about to happen. Before he could get the words out of his mouth, "Not yet, Livey!" Olivia blurted, "This one?" She pressed the button, and the blender began to gurgle and shake. Startled, Olivia jumped back. Peepa quickly told her to hold down the lid. She lunged forward to grab the handle and hold down the lid but pushed the blender sideways, knocking the lid off. The blender was now spewing chunks of grape skins and juice, blasting a purple mess all about the kitchen. By the time her grandfather could shut the blender off and place the lid back on it, there were purple spots on the kitchen floor, Olivia's mixing table, and some of the cabinets. It looked like a grape bomb had exploded in the kitchen.

Disaster Recovery!

"Oh no, Peepa. What are we going to do?" cried Olivia.

"Time for an emergency cleanup," responded her grandpa. "But first, wash off the purple goo on your face and arms." He quickly grabbed a bucket and a couple of mops out of the kitchen closet while Olivia went into the bathroom to wash up.

Olivia and Peepa were busy mopping the purple mess off the floor. He was scrubbing the table and the cabinets when they heard the door to the entrance at the bottom of the stairs open.

"Livey," said Peepa, speaking in a very low voice. "See if you can keep Mimi in the hallway while I clean up here."

"Okay, Peepa," whispered Olivia. She spun around and dashed out of the kitchen to intercept her grandmother in the hallway. "Hey, Mimi, I thought you were helping downstairs?" Olivia said, trying to act calm.

"I sure was, but now I want to see how things are coming along in my kitchen."

Olivia wasn't sure if Peepa was finished cleaning, so she stood in front of her grandmother like a roadblock. "Well, how about playing a game?" Olivia asked.

Mimi was beginning to think something was up. "Olivia, that sounds like fun, but aren't you supposed to help Peepa with his purple soup?" she asked. "Okay, then let's head into the family room to play a game."

But they would have to pass through the kitchen to get to the family room. "No, you can't do that!" Shouted Olivia. "I mean, we don't want to disturb Peepa. Let's play out here in the living room."

"Since you don't want to disturb Peepa, that's fine with me," Mimi replied. Before walking into the living room, she peered into the kitchen. Noticing a bucket with two mops in the far corner, she smirked and thought, "Hmmm, now I know why Peepa can't be disturbed," she thought.

Olivia dashed into the family room and grabbed a couple of board games that were kept in the back stairway to the bedrooms upstairs. She zipped back through the kitchen, looked at Peepa, and winked. He smiled, giving her a thumbs up for a good job keeping Mimi out of the kitchen.

Making Purple Soup!

Peepa was busy in the kitchen, while Olivia faithfully kept Mimi out of the kitchen playing board games. Her grandfather had finished cleaning up the countertops and cabinets and was now taking the grape pulp and mashing it in a strainer. He squeezed the grape juice out of the pulp, straining it into a new pot while removing the grape seeds. He repeated that over and over until the pot with the grape pulp was utterly empty. Mimi and Olivia could hear the whirl of the blender as he blended the rest of the grape skins.

Mimi looked at her granddaughter. "Why don't you go see how your grandfather is doing in the kitchen," she said, winking at Olivia, who raced into the kitchen.

"Hey Peepa, how is that soup of yours?' she asked.

"Well, come over here and take a look," responded Peepa. He put down his big wooden spoon and picked up Olivia so she could peer into the big pot.

"Look!" she exclaimed, "It's all purple. How did you do that? It was all green and brown a few minutes ago." He smiled at Olivia and, with a wink, sent her back to her grandmother. "Hey, Mimi, he is making purple soup!"

"Well, he is not finished yet, Livey," Mimi said.

"He's not?" Olivia said, so surprised.

"No, he isn't, but be patient, and very soon, you will see the purple soup," Mimi answered.

Minutes passed by slowly while Olivia and Mimi were working on a puzzle. But Mimi could see Olivia fidgeting, anxious to return to the kitchen. "Olivia," Mimi whispered, "Why don't you check in on Peepa?"

Olivia got up and quietly tiptoed into the kitchen as if she was a secret spy.

This time, she saw Peepa pouring a large measuring cup of what looked like brown crystals into the pot. While he was stirring, he looked out of the corner of his eye. "Livey, did you come in here so you can give a status report to your grandmother?" he asked.

"Hey, how did you know I was in the kitchen?" she asked. "What are you doing now, Peepa?"

"I could see a reflection on the silver pot, and I guessed it was you," he answered with a big smirk. "Now I'm adding raw sugar to the purple soup."

Hmmm, Olivia was wondering what kind of soup Peepa could be making. She walked out of the kitchen, shaking her head.

Mimi looked up and asked, "Livey, something wrong? You look troubled!"

"Mimi, do you ever put sugar in your soups?" Olivia asked.

"A little bit, but only in certain ones. Like the tomato basil soup Cam likes. Why?" Replied Mimi.

"Well, Peepa is pouring tons and tons of brown sugar into his soup," Olivia said, stretching her hands far apart as high and as low as she could stretch her arms.

Mimi chuckled at her granddaughter's expression. "I think Peepa has everything under control."

Purple Goo in a Jar

It was getting close to bedtime. Olivia was wondering if her grandfather would ever finish his soup. She walked into the kitchen to find him grabbing glass jars with big tongs to take them out of the pan of boiling water and placing them along with the jar lids on the counter to dry. "What are you doing now, Peepa?"

"I'm getting these jars ready, so I can keep my special batch of purple splendor inside of them." He raised his eyebrows up and down like a magician ready to play his next trick. "You go upstairs and get ready for bed. When you come back down, you can see what I've made."

Olivia turned around and went upstairs with Mimi to change into her pajamas and brush her teeth. Wearing a long face, she was worrying about Peepa.

"Livey, what is the matter this time?" Mimi asked, trying to keep a serious face.

"It's your husband," Olivia responded, "He's going to put all that purple soup in little jars. Why doesn't he just put it all in a big soup pot as you do?"

Mimi chuckled, "My husband? Who just happens to be your grandfather is just fine. Let's go downstairs to see what he has done."

Just as Olivia walked into the kitchen, Peepa called her over. "Alright, Olivia, come here and check out what we have here."

Olivia grabbed a chair and stood on it with Mimi's help.

This time, Peepa used a big soup ladle, not a wooden spoon. He grabbed an empty jar and dipped the ladle into the pot. Out came the ladle, and Peepa emptied it into the jar. But to Olivia's surprise, it was now a darker purple color; and it was thick and gooey, not runny or soupy.

"That doesn't look like soup to me!" exclaimed Olivia.

"You're so right, Livey. It doesn't. I wonder what happened." Peepa said, making Olivia believe he was just as surprised as her. "There's only one way to see what really happened." He took a teaspoon, dipped it into the jar, and held it out for Olivia to taste. "Now blow on it to cool it. It may be a little hot." She blew on the spoon as if she was blowing out five birthday cakes. Peepa said, "I think that should do it. Open wide for my big surprise."

Olivia grabbed the spoon and slurped up the purple goo. Her eyes popped open big and wide, her smile went from ear to ear, and she let out the loudest yummy sound a girl could give. "Peepa!" She cried, "You turned your purple soup into tasty grape jam."

There Is Plenty for All

The next morning, as Olivia came down the stairs, making her way to the kitchen, she could smell freshly made pancakes. Sure enough, a stack of golden-brown pancakes was waiting for one hungry girl. She looked over at the counter to see so many jars of dark purple jelly she could not count them all. Besides the jars of jam, there were some pots filled with leftover grapes from Peepa's vines in his backyard. "Hey, Peepa!"

"What is it, Olivia?" Peepa asked.

"You didn't use all the grapes to make your jam," said Olivia sounding disappointed.

"No, I did not. You know, sometimes it's much easier to snack on a hand full of grapes than to grab a jar of jam and spread it on toast," explained Peepa. Looking over his reading glasses, with a grin on his face, he said, "Come over here and let me tell you something you need to know before we devour those pancakes that you've been eyeballing since you walked into the kitchen."

Olivia walked over and sat next to her granddad. Looking up at Peepa, she asked, "What can be more important than eating those delicious pancakes?"

Ignoring her question, he approached the pan of grapes, took one, cut it in half, and walked back to the table. "Let me tell you what this seed can do. Plant it, and you get a grapevine, as we have in the backyard. Remember all the clusters of grapes we saw a few months ago? Better than one vine, we have four grapevines that provide shelter for bird nests together. And not only have we been snacking on them, but so have the birds, the bees, and the squirrels, just like we saw this past summer. The vines also kept us dry as an umbrella when we got summer rain. Finally, anyone who entered the yard, whether by air, from the trees, or on two feet, snacked on the grapes, and we still had plenty to make all that jam."

Olivia looked up at her Peepa. "I forgot all about those things," she said. "I never realized how so much can happen from little seeds."

"And you were so worried about the snow and our little robbers sneaking in the backyard." Peepa looked at her. "Olivia, that all came from just our backyard. Imagine all the grapevines in this city, in our state, in our country, and around the world. Isn't God a good provider for so many? And we're just talking about grapes. You know, Olivia, grapes are very important to God's story for you and me."

Olivia looked at the jars of jam. "They are?"

"Sure, they are. Grapes, grapevines, and juice from the grapes are mentioned over 400 times in The Bible," he explained.

"FOUR HUNDRED TIMES!" She shouted.

"Easy Livey, you're going to wake up your great grandparents." He chuckled at her surprised reaction. "Yes, that many times. Remember how upset you were with me for pruning the vines? Jesus uses the same example of how God, in a sense, prunes our lives."

Olivia immediately pulled her arms and hands close to her body, asking with a look of horror, "Why would He do that?"

Peepa looked at her, trying not to laugh, "No, silly. He would never prune your body parts. God takes away things in our lives that would prevent those who love Him and trust Him from getting closer to Him."

"Ooohh, I get it. Like when I need to spend more time with mommy and daddy than I do playing with my toys and games," remarked Olivia. "That's right. Something just like that, Olivia." Peepa responded. "Well, we can't let these warm pancakes sit on our plates."

"No, we cannot, Peepa. But where is the syrup?"

"Hmmm, I have a better idea," Peepa got up, grabbed a teaspoon, and opened a new jar of grape jam.

They gave thanks to God for all His provisions.

Olivia spooned out great globs of purple and smeared the jelly all over her pancakes. Every bite left a big purple ring around her mouth. After every bite, she ran her tongue around the outside of her mouth, licked off the jelly, and smacked her lips while making a long, yummy sound.

Appendix: Peepa's Purple Soup Recipe

Peepa's Grape Jam
Materials & Ingredients

Wooden pestle (if using grapes with seeds)	**Metal strainer** (if using grapes with seeds)
Two large pots (if using a significant number of grapes with seeds)	**Strainer** (for washing/rinsing grapes)
Bowls (for storing pulp & skins)	**Wooden spoons**
Ladle	**Blender**
Stove-Oven mitts or gloves	**Candy thermometer**
8 oz. mason jars	**Tongs**
Home grown or farmer's market grapes	**Brown raw cane sugar**

Note:

- Raw cane sugar (16 oz for every 5 lbs. of grapes) $1/20^{th}$.

  Using the grape skins reduces the need of sugar.

- Approximately two 8 oz. mason jars for each pound of grapes.

- Variety type of grapes can be used at the same time if desired.

Peepa's Grape Jam

- Allow time to sterilize jars ahead of time. Submerge jars & lids in boiling water for 10 minutes. Using tongs remove jars, lids and seals to dry in a rack.
- Discard partially eaten, bad or unripen grapes.
- Rinse Grapes.
- Separate grape pulp from skins into two bowls.
- Refrigerate pulp/skins if not cooking them at one time.
- Place pulp in pot under a low flame to soften pulp. Stir them until they are soft and squishy.
- For grapes with seeds- Scoop seeds into a metal strainer in a separate pot. Mash pulp with a pestle until all pup and juice is squeezed into pot. Clean out strainer and repeat process until all the grape pulp is separated.
- Puree grape skins and pour into pot with the grape pulp and juice.
- Bring the stove to a medium flame. Stir contents to avoid sticking to the pot.
- Continue to puree skins and mix raw sugar gradually into the pot as you add more pureed skins.
- Bring heat to a level where it reads a temperature of 220 F or 104 C on the thermometer. Continue to stir to avoid sticking or burning the content to the bottom of the pot.
- As contents thicken, scoop out the thicker contents into jars wearing oven gloves. Lower temp to avoid burning. Repeat the process until all contents are in jars. Increase heat when necessary. Leave approximately a ¼ inch space at the top of the jar when filling jars.
- Seal jars with lids. Place them upside down in a pan of water with jars have submerged. Boil water for 10 minutes. Remove jars with oven gloves and tongs right-side up. Ensure lids are tightly sealed. Repeat until all jars have been processed.
- Let jars cool to touch before storing.
- Refrigerate once a jar is opened for consumption.

"I am the true vine,"

The words of Jesus of Nazareth

- Gospel of John Chapter 15

Scan the QR code for more on Bill's books.

Made in the USA
Monee, IL
03 April 2026